RIPPLES IN SILENCE

TAMALI NEOGI

Transcendent Zero Press

Houston, Texas

ISBN: 978-1-946460-77-6

RIPPLES IN SILENCE

TAMALI NEOGI

Foreword

Contrary to many contemporary poetry publications, as well as modern painting and music compositions, the latest poetry collection of Tamali Neogi has a very personal signature and offers a large variety of themes. Many poems refer to Indian mythology and invite Western readers not only to read more about Hinduism and Buddhism, but also to read the works of the great Indian poet Rabindranath Tagore to whom Tamali Neogi refers several times. But as the present poetry presumes, Tamali Neogi studied also Greek and Roman cultures as well as the Bible. Some of the poems refer also critically to the present as in the poem **Disease of Unhappy Times:** "like famine to a blasted city, / appears on my threshold, / a disease of unhappy times / when corruption fuels violence, / justice likened to a forgotten myth". Or in another poem "Chaos is not simple disorder, / chaos is much more, / Prometheus, the victim of injustice / your demand is justified, / but now defender has become offender, no hope". In the poem **The Joystick** she asks what our movements controls, if the joystick is the voice of the Lord what is knowledge, wisdom, in the face of steady decline and she asks: "Machine driven men and women, where's the time for dear ones?"

But also nature is very present in the poetry collection as well as love, including for her father and mother as in the poem **Yellow Joy:** "The little beauties like golden stones / sparkle on Mother's aanchal (the decorative end of a saree that metaphorically signifies shelter, protection, sanctuary) the aroma of bottled fragrance / used to sweeten the princess' dream… Mother's affection hangs around my neck, / I get lost / in the realm of yellow joy".

For Tamali Neogi, poetry is her hunger, “gnawing the best minds for a possibly best world” .

She invites us to leave our materialistic world to go to the world of innocent smiling children, where truth to beauty is fragrant, like soul to heart. Especially for Western readers, the present book not only offers fascinating poetry, but is also an invitation to Indian mythology and oriental values.

Here is a poet who negotiates archetypal human emotions and probes deep into the human unconscious to logically perceive the roots of human behaviour. Her poetry will impel the readers to interrogate if the feelings become alive in the poetically created magic house or do the generated feelings urge one to philosophically grasp the world of ideas.

Germain Droogenbroodt
elpoeta@point-editions.com

Germain Droogenbroodt is an internationally appreciated poet. So far he has written 17 poetry books, published in 30 countries. He is also a translator, publisher, and promoter of modern international poetry. He is the founder and editor of the Belgian publishing house POINT Editions, co-founder and advisor of JUNPA (Japan Universal Poets Association), general counsel of the Chinese cultural Association Huifeng, International Shanghai and founding president of the Spanish cultural foundation ITHACA. Germain Droogenbroodt has received many international poetry awards and was recommended for the Nobel prize of Literature 2017.

CONTENTS

Charade

What is it that belongs to me?
The birth fixed by some other powers,
death nails the utter non-belongingness
within a coating of peace -
the final reward, deliverance from
the agonies of dark nights,
restorative sleep ends the phase of fretful fever.

Wife, husband, children or dear ones,
or middle-aged clowns!
just visit your parents
abandoned in some undiscovered planet.
The cold simply freezes!
Oh no. It lulls you to sleep
inside a million years old factory,
owned by dementia, supreme,
sleep that walks you to new destinations.

What is yours when
each moment awakens you to new realties!
Peace comes when you know the bonds,
only as lessons in detachment!
Counts for little,
you claim them or disown.
Shall I now love my self,
my own authentic self!

Much to Say…

So much to say
yet very little can be uttered.
Remember you, mother,
in thirst one digs a hole on earth,
a deep hole perhaps,
for water level has gone downwards,
like our raw emotions
when alien growth
overshadows blood kinship.
But your child is puzzled,
what to say?
Someone says: "scoop out the muddy water,
keep the sediment out,
all that have made the pool of your
daughterly emotions murky".
Swayed by gallons of pure water, clean,
trapped in the whirlpool of emotions,
Mom, it's puzzling.

Elder daughter of a family,
your house, last in a blind lane
that beggars avoid,
ashamed of asking alms.
He in asylum,
morning spent in hope,
the evening brings a bread for each,
yet persists the passion for studies,
the siblings rarely understand
feelings of the elder girl.

Mom, I ask,
what brings the greatest calamity ever,
hunger or love?

Married, the first nuptial night,
like the Greek Fate, ordains.
"Children are my only bliss"!
Pushed to a corner,
offence and disregard,
yet you jotted down the poem
I was to recite the next day.

How so thankful to Him, mom?
He bestows the learning on you!
Indifference and ingratitude
define your daughter and son.
Time unfolds different truths for all.
When useless feelings
like the ink from a fountain pen,
spill all over,
inner mind like the blotting paper absorbs;
dry eyes become wise and friendlier.
Sympathy and regrets morph into liquid
as the river flows underground.

I remember the evening, the bookshop,
as flawlessly mom copied the poems
for daughter to learn,
genesis of a poem,
or intimations on failures
become hieroglyphics of poetry,
mother or daughter,
what more to say, mom?

Don't mind if I Say

Gentlemen,
Do you know me?
Don't mind if my irrepressible beauty
comprises complexion bequeathed by dusk,
the whiteness of nails
proffered by friendly swans for ages.
My winsome smile like the lovely *Kunda* flower
generates waves of envy in you.
as in each of your nerve I bloom
like the flower of passion, Red Oleander.

From *muladhara*, *kundalini* energy shoots upward,
Passion confined in the cave,
frees and prances around.
My body and mind get intertwined
as passion goes berserk,
often it recoils into the inkpot,
slithers into my silvery pen
when I write letters to *Ranjan*.

When *Tilotamma* hides in the temple,
you come as *Jagat Singh*.
Ranjan, you madden the Egyptian princess.
But for me your love seems to be boundless.
To fulfil my dream of freedom for all,
you, like a mad horse of rebellion,
run across *asumadrahimachal.*
I come out, standing on the threshold,
when your triumph is transfixed in my *bindi*
I give my all – affection and warmth.

But when the revolutionaries fail,
I burn my fine clothes, my books.
I adopt non-cooperation.

When disillusioned self earns freedom,
religious riots dare to tear my breasts,
Ranjan, you dare the rioters.
The dark woman, wooden faced,
stands by the window,
Our *Nikhilesh* or *Ranjan* never come back.
The curse of dead youths,
shall I say, dead theories burst upon the nation?
Bishu asks me, “when will our dreams come true
and the system change?”

Bishu, will you get me fresh flowers?
Bishu, you say, "As music to the hollow of the flute...”,
Bishu, you weep!
But I see no tears,
It’s our brown world where springs have gone dry,
Ha! The corporate greed of Leviathan!
He sucks up the juice of moral values.
as gods have always summoned the woman in crisis.
Ranjan, you need me.

I will induce the king to free you,
Mass is as powerless as innocent ripples,
when sunlight reflects in water waves,
mermaids smile in joy,
as sunlight, the flowing necklace of white opal,
adores their pristine beauty,
like the ribbons of diamond dust
that embrace the night sky
in the polar regions of Earth.
Yes, now the king understands.
In his new regime,
power won't be like the light that dazzles
but compulsive moonlight,
that adds to beauty.
Gentlemen, do you know, who am I?

**Kunda - a Bengali word, name of a white flower*
**Muladhara- "root support" or "root of existence" in Sanskrit*
**Kundalini- "a spiritual energy or life force located at the base of the spine" (Google)*
**asumadrahimachal- a Bengali word that refers to India in its entirety*
**bindi - a coloured dot worn on the centre of the forehead by Hindus, Jains, Buddhists from the Indian subcontinent*
**Nikhilesh, Ranjan, Bishu, Tilottama, Jagat Singh-characters from the writings of Tagore and Bankim Chandra Chattopadhyay*

A Miracle Man!

It was in nineteenth century,
as servant steals the ring of the master,
a white horse rider of the red dwarf
stole a molecule of hot plasma
and by some godly trick
placed it in the womb of a mother fortunate.
The child was born in hot summer
A miracle man!

Such is thy immortal glory,
that I, in love tremendous,
fresh as green beanstalk in sunny morning,
emotions as strong as giant whirlpools
of Northern Sea swirling in tandem,
have been waiting for centuries,
as you Victoria,
in the farthest corner of an unknown land,
as a flower in full bloom,
wait in silence for appreciation.

Come poet, come
come again to purify human affairs,
politics, international image,
come to conquer every form of art
through the power of visionary eyes
unravel to the lesser ones,
the mystery of thy creativity,
Semi-god like.

Come, poet, come
for when you don't sing the song of love,
and enliven the world with thy music,
our structures stand like
hollow wooden flutes, mere playthings.
Your melody can only free us,
our King from his self-imprisonment.
Come and sing like wind in Autumn
What else may teach him
to protect Mother for our sustenance?

Come, take modest offerings of my poor heart
an unschooled teenage girl sulking in grief.
Like my teacher, the Postmaster
now I too know how to philosophize
as *Chitrangada*, *Shama* or *Nandini,*
sisters to me, just different selves.
With me *Bouthan* has shared her
mountain like *aviman*.
Come, take me in thy embrace,
The New Woman born of century old learning!

Oh, mighty god!
You cover the entire terrain
riding seven chariots.
in darker times
bless us once more,
send thy son to this bleak house
as through the power of his pen
a new world may be reborn.
We are waiting for you,
the Miracle man!

**Victoria -Victoria Ocampo, Argentine critic and writer whom Tagore met in 1924*
**Postmaster, Chitrangada, Shama, Nandini- characters from Tagore's writings*
**Bouthan - a Bengali word that refers to Tagore's sister-in-law, wife of Jyotirindranath Tagore*
**Aviman - a Bengali word indicating a sense of perceived hurt so far as self-respect and personal worth are concerned*

Only Waiting

Everything comes to an end.
Man, you undress in my presence,
my postmodern lover!
In the darkness of the cave your forefathers grin.
In some moods you certainly like the female gaze.
As is beauty to a sensuous poet,
an impetus to creation,
doesn't feminine appreciation,
impinge on your senses,
a strong urgency of fornication?

A garter snake is secreting pheromones,
but my body feels no hunger,
it's not that what happens to an overfed animal
but as prolonged starvation blunts the senses
springs of the brain gone dry,
the body dies gently.

It's a generation of dysfunctional genitals,
though hyperactive brains,
I told my love the other day.
His kisses pierce my navel,
I read obituary of my small ovaries.
Everything comes to an end,
what remains is only waiting.

Tale of a Princess

From old manuscripts I know
of a princess asleep
for three hundred years or more.
She and her doctor,
a curse perhaps!
Who will tell me
what happens when they wake up!
So, I imagine
the princess's body and the doctor's brain,
remain unaltered,
then what follows is a love affair.

Youthful body and the brilliant brain,
what's common in the uncommon?
What connects a man to the earth he walks?
Two true minds dream together.
The old body sees through young eyes
the youthful body channelized by a hyperactive head,
a planet and the Sun, the unequals.

Have you heard
about the magic fruit of this strange union?
I didn't know before the evening
they touch the old tree in their garden.
Branches dried and shrunk,
What disease, who knows?
But what's that?
Two new leaves sprouting fanned by the wind! Wah!

Himself living through challenging terrains
yet a true devout prays for all,
blessed are those whose love is genuine!
But from that day
the body and the brain start to decline.
No idea, why?
Love, the artist, creates masterpiece
on the canvas of our life
The ultimate is good
though the present staggers and falls.

Firki

Wandering in the green regions on an evening
cerebral larva crawls into my numb brain
nibbles at the tree of my sensibility,
flies away to some unknown region,
for the savage world of deadly traps
conveys Firki is selected for *Kumari Pooja.*

Her father is the toilet cleaner,
equality is no longer a mere dream!
The butterfly dances around my ears
the music of her flapping wings,
inundates my afflicted world with hope.

Wandering aimlessly,
a thought just crosses my mind.
Will it rain today?
Suddenly I am alone.
Where have you gone?
My butterfly, stamping your beauty upon society,
are you waiting for the day,
when you will add more colour to rainbow?

Choking darkness reminds me of you, Firki
are you not the girl, raped several times,
in the backside *jhopdi* of Southern Avenue
now set out for some remote valley of Amazon?
Butterfly, you never returned!
Only rain comes occasionally
to save this godforsaken earth!

**Kumari pooja - a Hindu ritual observed during Navaratri or Durga Puja wherein young girls (between 2-10) are worshipped as embodiments of goddess Durga, signifying the recognition of feminine power and the importance of respecting girl children*

**Jhopdi - hut.*

No Alternative

Mother you die
shielding us from difficulties
though we value little,
as from childhood to adulthood
it's just a happy jump,
pleasurable indeed.

Steadily or unsteadily
we walk along the known and untrodden paths.
Sometimes it is tightrope walking,
at times rock climbing,
sans monotony
for the natural dose of twists and turns.

Challenges like hunger never leave us
dreams force us to hop
as does kangaroo,
while it runs.
we do so,
at times stumble on the runway,
to avoid massacre.

But it's a three hundred sixty degree somersault
as we reach old age.
Now we remember you, mother
God saves those who confess their flaws
albeit learn the hard way against odds!

It's the same story of prodigal son.

Yellow Joy

That day I lost my path in a jungle
where little nameless flowers
held me tightly to their soft chests.
As a postman searches for an address,
I too tried to fathom a strange sensation,
yet know you not!

The little beauties like golden stones
sparkle on Mother's *aanchal,*
the aroma of bottled fragrance
used to sweeten the princess' dream
but that of a mild incense,
the farmer's wife burns, and the smile
that lights up her wrinkled face
cannot be purchased through millions,
but the gleam on the child's face
like the morning rays through the window,
becomes his sister's joy.
Mother's affection hangs around my neck,
I get lost
in the realm of yellow joy.

**aanchal - the decorative end of a saree that metaphorically signifies shelter, protection, sanctuary*

First Priority

When I loved my classmate,
all pounced on me, focusing on his imperfections,
the hatred my brothers had for him,
was just like what the impotent king had
for the most seductive nigger.
He traps and forces himself on him.
He is our guard of the most beautiful queen.

When I love a teacher,
he demands me to change;
Earth has always surrendered to the sea
that knows not to look back.
Never the same again
when recedes the flood of love.

When I love a critic,
to him me and my body
are areas of investigation!
Then I begin to love myself,
a million times stronger than a man,
reconstructive phase after Tsunami,
see how beautifully energetic I am,
rising above the clouds, catching the tail of a comet,
and fly into zones defying gravitation!
I enjoy the swing,
relaxingly on the rod of lightning,
waiting for the world to know
what happens when a woman
begins to prize herself!

It's Peace Now

The ardour of a lover scales high
when unsure of his beloved's fidelity,
like our perception of *maya* with growing age.
To live for him, to live for her,
Alas! It's an injury prone world.

As frogs when the rule of water prevails or
ghosts during the new moon,
can you be sure of the best season
for fungi or virus?
The watery sponge easily removes
the child's writ on the slate.
What's so serious about it?
Penetrating through the pores of my frame
the invisible bodies dance lightly,
as the helpless other silently enters the coffin.

I have seen him in the market,
an older man,
fighting with a bull,
for a piece of rotten watermelon.
Back to primitiveness!
Yet I wonder why not insanity,
a blessing, a privilege at times,
in a world of colossal confusions
and immense complications.

Why not dear?
Insulated from thousand injuries,
offences and cruelties,
the deranged battalion moves on,
to be lost in the crowd,
the paraphernalia of human resource,
It's peace now.

Buried lie the crazy queen and her Roman lover,
obscured by years of mountainous blames.
What's so serious about it?
So, in darkened face,
my light soul sits and reads
laughs and gossips,
for I know, suffering damp and dark,
can break my organic matter,
but once I stop sympathizing with myself,
it will vanish in shame!
Peace now.

Father's Wish

Haven't you heard
the latest gossip of the year?
A damned woman was she
who lost life playing with emotions.
All say it's absurd, but yes, finally
she fell in love with a man
who grows into a stoic,
a venerated rock,
sacred stone,
witness to forgotten history.

Wise as a Rishi in Vedas
Noah or Abraham or the father
who pardons his lost lamb!
Strange machinations, indeed!

Soon the lady gets lost in her jewellery,
the most captivating mistress of cravings,
frivolity utmost but why not?
for she must be in her best as he comes.
The little one,
a wish to hide her flaws and ignorance,
under the cushion of false glory.
Beware! His wish.

Like the monsoon cloud spoiling
the prospects of a sunny morning,
strange affliction darkens her skin,
kills the good blood cells fast.
The goldsmith by one stroke
transforms her into an unalloyed gold needle
to sew his gaping wounds!
What is wisdom? Going beyond misery or
how to organize oneself?

Look at the garland Father dear wears today,
his pain condensed in the beads,
whereas her devotion,
forms the locket
of His floral necklace.
Strange Indeed!

Monsoon Love

When worries subside
in its intricate pattern,
the spectacular beauty of peacock's feathers,
when in monsoon trees smile through tears
being not allowed to flow in the hottest month,
when muddy earth succumbs
to the plough of the sickly farmer.

When crossing miles in dark,
unpredictable mood of the cloudlet,
becomes the lovers' sole concern,
when waiting is most painful
on the dismal evenings,
raging sea matches the pride of the storm,
then come to me silently,
like the petals of *kamini* on dark nights,
jasmine saturated love
seeps into the hushed breath of lovers.

As the divine droplets pour from the sky
on the ardent lovers and vulnerable minds,
wash away the ugly sensations
from the smitten hearts,
to pave the way and convey
Monsoon love is for all!

**Kamini - Bengali name for a fragrant white flower*

Your Voice I Hear

A chronological narrative of past and present
washed over with consciousness of pain,
when loving father is on deathbed;
powerful force of paternal bond
overturns equations.
Preposterous. Why can't we
relive our past?
Existence is mocked
by towering waves of fresh pain.

Father, you are now a bundle of bruised nerves,
deep veins blue in pain,
as doctors fight to stabilise the vitals,
trembling lips say 'Relax'.
Life sap drains out,
as the pale faces of children pain the father!
Ah!

Why is there so much suffering, Lord?
The hangman is grinding his teeth,
yet alive!
Is there any dream hidden mischievously,
under his broken ribs?
Life takes all that it gives,
does it care how we trade in?
Lord, spare me! Action must supersede feeling!

Perhaps we are strange species,
stubborn, unlikely to learn.
A planet that rotates around itself,
also revolves around the Sun.
We create new bonds,
welcome strangers
to the warm hearths flaming in our hearts.
But Man, do you repay your loan to elders?
Thankless we walk forward,
ungrateful mammal, same is our lot,
as on the final day the two ends converge.
Father if I am with you, it's your love, not mine.

So when I call you,
Deep sadness come,
sit on my eyebrow and
chew up the threads of my agonized state,
it's your voice father that I hear,
'Relax'.

Magic or Mystery

A dream is a dream, amazing!
Last night they came,
an old woman with a magical pot of water,
descends from a mysterious source,
which fount and amazing cave?
every time she drinks it empty,
with magical residues left.

The other is an old man, thousand years of age,
Wow! His pen is like the magician's wand.
And see its marvellous power,
his age-old lines,
exude the beauty of a new bride!
Is it a mystery? Amazing!
It is our world where everyone claims
he is the best,
but a dream is a dream.
A short story and a poem nearly lost
looking at each other in dazed silence!
What will you say?

The Epiphanous Moment

The Guru asks his disciple
"What is the most meaningful thing in the world?"
Ten years past in search;
conclusions scrupulously reached
either oversimplified or overstated.
Sad!
Then comes the epiphanous moment.
He wonders why does the guru say it so often
"dance of dolls is the ultimate metaphor of life?"
As during the puppet show,
the string responds to fiat of the puppeteer.

Someone is rotating the finger
clockwise or anticlockwise,
at every point of the movement,
a day is unfolded in new colour, a cyclic pattern,
as rotates the earth
so moves this globe of colour!

The inhabitants know for sure
it's the colour of actions, inactions or reactions,
painting our feelings and emotions; auto-filled.
The disciple says to himself,
happiness or sadness are mere signifiers
in the grand fest of life.
But not the same, the
ceaseless flux of experience,
it's God.
The guru smiles as he overhears.

The Best Landlord

Mind, the landlord shows no judgement
while accommodating the tenants.
A statement only!
When King and poet occupy adjacent rooms,
it is natural that they fight.
except when the poet is dressed as a sweet fool.

The grand self boasts
the humble one just listens endlessly!
No, not always.
"Sir, you build monuments that collapse,
like crowns made of egg shells,
but with images and symbols,
I constructed Paradise,
blissful, eternal".
The *Fakir* says: "Who is decidedly humble between us?"
The poet must be like Shakespearean fool.

Hundred arguments in defence of each,
the landlord tolerates it all.
Finally, what works is the owner's plea for peace.
Mind is such a landlord who accommodates all.
A statement only. But what about the inner conflicts?
Who is free to listen to the bitter fool?
Stop. Some other tenants have started fighting.
Mind is the best landlord who judges none.

**Fakir- a Muslim or Hindu ascetic who lives solely on alms*

Give Me a Hug

Old, too weak to move,
Sherry, I live your pain
in the silent patterns of crippling agony.
No expectations, no hope;
in the moist mirror of your eyes,
I see motifs of waiting for the last hour,
our Sherry is going to marry death.

When you last crawled onto my lap,
I may be mistaken,
you can't speak my language,
no engagement in abstract thought,
yet someone whispers into my ears:
"Father, don't weep. Togetherness is both body and mind".
Like the stars,
steadily shining in the day!

Wet eyes, bleeding hearts, separated lovers,
the dear ones, the mad planets
will soon be consumed
in exhaustive rotation.
Old, too weak to move,
daughter, pardon a helpless father,
Bidaai won't be ceremonious
but he promises/prophesies
she will assume luminous motifs of holy art,
and chill of the world won't scare.
Come on dear, give me a last/warm hug!

**Bidaai- refers to the traditional Indian wedding ceremony wherein the bride leaves her parental home to start her married life*

My Mood

As shadows looms over the evening,
mood sulks
over the imperfections littered around.
When deep sighs crack the earth,
I look up to sky but
who knows that the owl
ponders over the same question
I was about to ask Moon –
what is perfection?
But no one believed the answer
conveyed through quaking of earth!

That day while the Sun was rising upwards
from the debris of skyscrapers,
the red light was waking up the sleeping stars,
dead crows hanging from the electric wires,
I gaze at the harmonious natural world
amid the infirmities of centrifugal forces,
where even gods are not free.
Relaxingly, my mood intones
"Perfection is a hypothesis constructed imperfectly" .
Then the reason whispers
"Perfection like others is also context dependent".

Free of Hawkers

What fits us most
Other than the election slogans
during the cruellest months of Summer?
It's like an invisible force
driving the bullock cart aimlessly across barren heath,
that lies flat beneath the singeing Sun.

That evening with permission from the old Sun,
I plead with the hypocrite Moon
for lulling to sleep the basic concerns,
to peep into the kitchen of hawker Rama Singh,
through the hole in our backyard wall.

Yes! The moon stops smiling unnecessarily,
the mother is boiling rice and potato
soon the curry will be prepared for
the son's starving liver and the mother's intestine!
As the loud speakers atop vehicle promise
the city will be free of hawkers,
the largest propaganda of the ruling party!

Despair! Despair!

Evil is offending, evil cataclysmic,
Hence mythological punishment
for those who bring chaos back!
Chaos is not simple disorder,
chaos is much more,
Prometheus, the victim of injustice
your demand is justified,
but now defender has become offender,
no hope. Despair, despair!

An image of brutalized doctor
haunts the Nation's eternal sleep,
from her siesta, Bharat Mata rises up,
singing a song!
"Yet no one is found guilty!
No hope. Despair, despair,
Man’s backbone is the cheapest commodity,
in this grand fair
where stock declares human values to be low-priced
trade items. cheers!
Lo Lo! Despair, despair.
Now my battered soul
will sing the song,
till you come, my sons
strip me off my honour,
my legs and hands are manacled,
Lo Lo! Despair, despair.

Tear off my ring finger,
segregate my body parts,
come on, stab me,
take out my eyeballs,
for I have birthed you, bastards.
Lo! Lo! Despair, despair.
Blood splattered on my ears, face, and genitals,
dear ones, do one thing,
break my thyroid cartilage,
throttle me to death.
Come on my impudent sons,
you will soon be free
and lapped up for contesting elections!"

Evil, you are offending, cataclysmic,
yet Master of the masses!
Devis and *Devatas* dare not intervene
as the power-crazy groups run amuck
and sane counsels get drowned in the din
of fire-breathing patriots!

As people celebrate freedom and democracy
amidst false promises and ascending fears
one monotonous voice exhorts
"Go, Make her".
The eagle in condescending confusion
eats up the genitals of Prometheus!

No hope. Despair, despair!

**"Go, Make her"- in Mahasweta Devi's short story "Draupadi", the chief orders his army thus, insinuating that the woman protagonist be raped.*
** Devis and Devatas- female and male deities*

Poetry is Hunger

Sensitive conscious begs the subconscious
for a befitting picture
to have a dialogue with anarchy,
and conflicting emotions.
In a queue or at times haltingly,
come the images and shape themselves,
into the self-designed cage of elastic words.
Poetry is hunger,
peace eludes the artist's mind
as bleeds the beggar's belly, ever.
Appreciate the beauty of the full moon!
No, it's something more.
When you paint the Moon
with the agonies of a wretched soul,
and the big, heavenly dish relieves you of hunger,
you are a poet.

The moment I write this
a girl is getting tortured in my land.
Hungry is my mind
like the vagina of the earthy woman,
it ceases to be pigeonhole,
but mouth of volcano
eager to subdue power play of muscles.
Poetry is my hunger,
gnawing the best minds for a possibly best world.

My Nameless Sisters

The evening I envisioned my deserted, forsaken selves
sitting on the dried petals of the withered rose,
thoughts of withdrawal or idea of resignation,
what might have brought them together?
I simply wonder.

Friends in misery speak like me
the nameless sisters,
sleepless spirits know the truth,
how we relive the pain as
demons are free to break our pelvis joints,
our neck bones,
and legs torn apart!

Sitting on the petals of a withered rose,
I see my fractured dreams moaning,
maybe they have the vision,
this year *Devi Mata* won't grace our land,
justice it is,
for demons lose their powers
worshipping the lifeless idols,
an age, nearing apocalypse.

My deserted, forsaken selves,
smile a little but don't hope,
don't tell me in hushed voice,
to wait now for honest men and true lovers!

**Devi Mata - goddess Durga*

Disease of Unhappy Times

Disease of Unhappy Times
like famine to a blasted city,
appears on my threshold,
a disease of unhappy times
when corruption fuels violence,
justice likened to a forgotten myth.

Look, do the creases on my forehead
look like signposts of the untrodden paths,
where hundreds of bodies will be piled up?
A vulgar display! Or a tribute to brutal power!
A little distance away – is the chemo factory
where they burn cancerous cells,
yes, I have heard.

My bowels have turned upside down
like the villages before aerial attack,
welcome, Death, come and play
with my intestines like the rapist of *Nirbhaya*,
let me "cry blood".
Ah! What stops you?

Kiss my face, the graveyard,
natural forces have wrought integral designs
after the white gowns declare me cold.
Foxes have perhaps got the scent
let them flake me off
like the skin of a deserted city.
Goodbye.

**Nirbhaya - a girl who is brutally raped (afterwards she dies in hospital) in New Delhi in 2012*

**"cry blood"- a reference to R.G.Kar incident in Kolkata. The rapist throttles the on-duty lady doctor so forcefully that blood oozes out of her eye balls.*

You Came to Me

You came to me,
travelling along the roads,
washed by tears, sapphire droplets,
pure emotions of a subdued angel,
love of a disturbed century,
waiting years in vain,
to hold you in *shiuli* breasted embrace,
the day you came to me.

Drowning your discomfort,
in the ocean of my absolute piety,
stands alone thy dear one,
not as the *Shala* tree in a dry forest,
rather a beggar in a lonely lane,
wondering at your commitment.

Uncanny silence pervades,
I question, is it a dream of a world
where a star is burnt by its own fire,
like truth lost in the search?
Here melodrama qualifies.

Or the day,
all lies start revolting
against oppression of the white sisters
the day you came to me!

** shiuli - Bengali word for night-flowering jasmine*
** Shala- Shorea robusta, the sal tree, is a species of tree native to India, Bangladesh, Nepal, Tibet and across the Himalayan regions (Google).*

A Fool Was I

A fool was I,
opening my heart to the frosty air,
when snowflakes adorned my hair,
like a dove, spread my wings more and more,
welcome changes,
almost to discover a new woman in myself,
innocent was my black, hairy body,
yet who will convince my Victorian lover?
Tess dies umpteen deaths!

"A fool was I",
soliloquizes the smallest flower,
"to take kindness of rain for bliss.
Where is the skylark to guide me?
Kindness is not love,
perhaps the last song is sung;
I am undone".

“A fool was I”,
cries the restless air, heavy with charcoal,
white skinned, black masked,
who will console her?
The ghostly things of earth prefer confusion.
Flapping sounds of the crude wings of ugly bats
say, “Cheers!”
when not far away, wood catches fire.
In the huskiest voice,
wandering souls of the nestlings,
tiny creatures, dead before they mature to die,
thoughtfully whisper into my ears,
Innocence is sin!

How much fool was I!

Lady of the Mountain Villa

When pregnant clouds prematurely birth deep melancholy,
when jasmine flowers kiss the grass palette gently
when in dark nights, wind sings the saddest song,
a benumbing pain from my naval shoots upward,
tearing my chest into numerous lumps,
is it then that I miss you?

A friend real, a companion of forty years,
the lady of this mountain villa,
standing on the terrace, year after year,
prays for my well-being, my long life!
Alas!
When preordained suffering robs warmth of granny
I join the bookworms on lonely nights,
chewing through books, collected in multitudes,
what is knowledge,
what wisdom
in the face of steady decline,
the ancient fear?

Some husbands, my dear,
are loyal to their soulmates,
years after they depart.
When silence makes mockery
of the words said and unsaid,
and promises ruptured,
when the lowly moon
alights on the roof of portico,
is it then that I miss you, dear lady?

**saree - a dress particularly worn by Bengali women from South Asia*

On an Errand

The Guru asks a lover first,
"who is god?"
The lover says:
"Our rocky faith in extreme goodness creates god,
as I have created her, my love,
no philosophy but ways of life bring one close to gods.
Life is a pilgrimage as are the pious ways of true love.
A glimpse is so fulfilling!
May He be god in the temple,
carved off stones in some deserted hilly region,
difficult to set foot in,
or be one's true love,
for whose loving touch,
a lifelong waiting is perhaps nothing".

At this point, the Guru poses same questions to a fresher.
"To me perfection is god,
as the aesthetic beauty of the palace of truth,
to poets, and to dancers, inimitable *Apsaras'* art", says he.

The Guru says:
Every night Earth puts on its back
the weight of a dark rucksack,
our sadness, sufferings, grievances,
but every morning infinite number of golden rays
light it up, opens floodgates of hope.
God is light.

The fresher and the lover are on an errand,
I hear they strive against faith to bag sunlight!!!

**apsara - in Hindu mythology, a celestial nymph*

Couldn't say it now

Couldn't say it now
that you don't love me
as you have done what insane lovers do,
when Camarillo,
the white horse goes berserk,
glaciers melt inside,
flooding the sewage of unwanted sentiments
that barricade the heavenly unison.

Heard of the strange tales,
mothers segregate their breasts from body,
to cook for the dying children in *76' monnontor*;
don't forget the flag wavers
whose bare feet
cross the mountains of thorns.
But perhaps the strangest thing is
when the most affectionate star
walks into the parlour of dusky evening,
holds the hand of this lonely queen of night,
asks, "So love, how are you?"

In her mind the queen wonders,
what can match his truthful love,
maddening is his fixity in a fickle world,
has she tried to know his worth?
She recounts . . .
The white interiors of his cold palace,
perhaps smells of unearthly devotion,
white soul ever awakened,
to multiple patterns of endless suffering….
He repeats the question as she is already lost!

The reverie continues.
"Where was I
when odour of death
threatened you to perspire,
when attacks of lonely hours,
wreaking havoc on you for a trillion of years,
when disruptive events crush your bones to dust,
when with tremendous control you held back,
the push towards the black hole,
the attraction, the gravitational force
which have shaken empires.
As me of you,
here sailors only accept the bounties of the sky".

Couldn't say it now
that you don't love me,
for your kisses have created a wonder,
never again will misery pierce the veil of love,
some mist will be hanging around me,
till comes the holy baby, the happiest morning ever.
Till then for God's sake
keep the eyes of the dusky queen awake,
for a glance at you, my brightest star!
Earth displays the hoarding splendidly,
"you are everywhere".

Couldn't say it now
that you don't love me
for you have . . .

**76' monnontor - Refers to the Great Bengal Famine of 1770, also known as Famine of 76 as it occurred during the Bengali year 1176*

The Dam Breaks

At the end of the day
it remains,
the stony truth,
the dissociating altitudes
between us,
the body aches,
but soul transcends.

What is beautiful in me
yearns to reach the ultimate.
In my heart
the dam breaks.
Let the flood
unify the dreams,
if not the dreamers.
Amen.

The Voice Inside

Empty nights chew me up,
days cause internal turmoil,
in the great *bazar* of hypocrites
where lie displays my particles,
packaged in multi-coloured hues.
What more?
A massacre of honour on vulgar display!
Come on, seal the lip,
Silence the inner voice fast!

**bazar - market*

Last Love

On that cloudy morning,
idle in my maiden balcony,
I asked my intimate friend,
looking deep into the blue eyes
of other worldly thoughts,
how will be my last love?
Say to me must, my darling Infancy.

A turmoil I felt in mind,
there's nothing called 'last love',
the philosopher's protests are silenced first.
Only then I hear a mellowed voice,
"In Last love you are *kash* looking upward,
scudding cloud beautiful,
figuring out the Presence vast,
mind and soul traversing across
the forest of unruly emotions.

Waiting for the sacred touch,
disguised in the end,
comes the divine in human form!"

**Kash - in English Kans grass flower. It's also known as Saccharum spontaneum, a type of white wild grass flower native to Indian subcontinent.*

Rainbow in Love

All frown,
sans her lover,
when the elderly bride
wears a dark red *Benarasi,*
after an eternal wait for a decade long!

Cheap cosmetics cannot hide
the wrinkles on her face;
like the cracks on my surface.
Lies camouflaged my hidden wish,
a momentary stay in the world of clouds,
fulfilment in rain!

The newly wed
arrives at her in-laws' place,
with a basket full of colours,
rainbow in love!!!
Ah! don't mock her sentiments,
else meaningless will be my efforts;
see how I look different in each hour of the day,
no grievances,
seek your love anew,
though dry is my skin, hazy my eyes,
colourless are my lips,
Evil has sucked my life blood and
I am left anaemic.

Yet if pale orange allures you, dear,
I am your evening sky,
If grey, I am dusk.
How many colours graced you *Ulupi*,
The night *Arujuna* gifts you ever?
Or as *Pujarini* at the feet of Buddha,
have your ascetic beauty secured you,
a triumph over the feminine craze, archetypal desire?

Till you reply,
let me be lost
in the bare chest of the sky,
let my tears kiss the lips of daylight,
in the world of afternoon hues,
rainbow, in love!!!

**Ulupi - a Naga princess, wife of Arjuna in Mahabharata*
**Arjuna -a heroic character in Mahabharata*
**Pujarini - a character who appears in Tagore's poem, "Pujarini"*

Under the Chatim Tree

My friend, will you please do me favour?
Ask him who has journeyed across space,
alien soil braving the agonies of the heart,
how many times he got lost
on similar roads diverging apart?
The question pumps my arteries
my swollen, blue vein like the finger of a child's skeleton,
writes on the walls of my heart,
"It's puzzling!"

After nine suspenseful days and nights,
covered in black soot from head to face,
the sailing soul returns
dark as evening in that thatched hut
where dreams are carelessly fractured
and candles are blown off
by the unforeseen storm.

Feelings in words flow from my lips
as the lovers under the *Chatim* tree,
kiss for the last time
before drifting to different worlds
weathering the seasonal ups and downs.
Chance meetings may bring back
parted friends, loving memories,
of the dears parted at the forked end of a road,
to meet again and part again
to defined destinations on the road of life!

**Chatim - Bengali of blackboard tree, scholar tree, milkwood tree, native to Southern China, Southeast Asia, Australasia.*

A Naughty 'No'

That night I couldn't sleep,
do you know why?
As I closed my eyes
I heard a naughty "no".

Sitting on a flying horse,
the girl is ready to ride,
across oceans, valleys and dales,
to reach her lover.
Who knows some short distances
get difficult to traverse!

Perhaps I was dozing off
yet she whispers into my ears.
I open my eyes widely.
Crossing the huge barren land,
the vast expanse, step by step,
she is advancing to the last barrier
between them.

Under a *Sonajhuri* tree stands
an old man with stooping shoulders
holding books to shrunken chest
waiting for his elusive Anima.
When two pairs of eyes meet,
a long-awaited treat
heart palpitates, feelings in spin
common sense drowned by strangers' grin.
Strangeness dissolved in loving embrace
as the girl is drenched in his grace.

Don't you ask me,
what happens after the girl meets her
lover?
Does her Pegasus start his journey to reach Olympus?
Believe me,
in the sweet sleep at night,
I hear a naughty 'No'.

**Sonajhuri - a fast-growing, crooked, gnarly tree in the family Fabaceae, native to Australia, Indonesia, Indian subcontinent and Papua New Guinea.*

Pure Woman

Pure woman, what causes your fall?
Difficult to describe, though easy to understand.
Please tell what squeezes your blood
love or lust?
Or contrived by the witch of loneliness,
whose throne is preserved in every Beauty's heart?
when love disheartens you, lust comes forward!
He gifts you the bouquet of roses, but
the thorn pricks your breast.

Sweetheart, don't you think
we are slightly misled,
as was the hesitant shrunk body
of your ideal lover?
The darkening of your skin,
the roughness of your hair,
sacrificial offerings to the hag,
loneliness, grand;
it is her machinations that
you got drowned in momentary confusion.

Just a second's failure,
yet destructive as poisonous overdose of pill,
swept away the queen of the unprotected lovely fort,
victory kisses the ministry of desire!
My dear, don't hate me if I say
though not in the whole,
Alex is creation of your confused heart,
My love, don't argue, just give in …

Who Suffers Most

Bloody hell! These daily conflicts!
Standing on the ground my Fancy sighs,
let me soar high,
little knows she,
soon the wistful mind,
lands on an uncharted terrain
as blows the rough wind of uneasy questions.

When a star and a planet fight, who suffers most?
Remember Krishna and *Kamsha*,
Radha knows the answer best,
Faceless women to be readily erased!
But when the battle is between father and lover
Juliet or Heer, what's the difference?
But when man and earth quarrel?

Ah! Please stop.
It's difficult to perceive
as if a wrestling match,
hot carbon emitted from one's breath
darkens the forehead of the other,
whose manoeuvre brings him to the mat.
Shall he now bribe the official,
to gloss over his illegal hold?
A corrupted mind is fit for a polluted world.
Oh! what a relief!
See at the end the wrestlers will stand
hand in hand.

My Fancy wishes to fly again,
La La La !

If I am Lost

Remember the evening I ushered you in,
the fair child of curly hair,
you crawled in straight,
without looking at or hearing me.
Where is your mom, dear?

Swimming across the mountain lake,
flooded with moonshine,
inattentive is the angel,
to the sights and sounds of our awkward life,
the great Master's Art,
the prothalamion to be eternally sung,
in marriage bond are this wondrous creation
and the arid world of fruitless actions,
where lies the meaning, dear?

Better to be in your own world,
in light or in dark, far different from ours,
in vain, the lesser beings judge the ways of God!
But dear,
diving deep into an unintelligible world,
if I am lost,
Stuart, my little child, hug me once.
Do not forget that evening,
I first opened my heart to you,
beginning of an uncompromising effort,
the angel, alien, guest to my lonely room.

Blank Eyes

Lost in the yellow world of full blossom,
valley of inordinate beauty,
reason flying like drunk grasshopper,
no coordination between the dancing nerves,
in inexpressive agony is lost man of nature,
blank eyes looking upward,
let Heaven interfere,
else, no *Desert Sage* in sandstorm,
fancy ceases to be nectar.

**Desert Sage -a hardy, aromatic perennial shrub native to the arid regions of the Western United States, prized for its drought tolerance.*

Similar Destination

Whatever the route I choose
to escape the trauma,
I reach the same destination,
as if in a dream, lost in a maze,
I croon the most desperate song ever.
Can you hear me?
Am I making an intelligible sound?
Don't know, don't know,
me too a stranger here.

Machine driven men and women,
Where's the time for dear ones?
Worry not if the babies too prefer their utopia,
for yours is a mechanical civilization.

The black child of the brick house,
unresponsive, puzzling,
as is dense fog on December morning,
to human efforts of fine solutions.
Whichever route I try to escape the trauma,
I reach the same destination.
Here curses bloom like daisies,
if you hear me, please respond.

No Wings to Fly

What new forms sanity may assume,
you will forever remember what I am going to say,
when to you, a man is turned into a big insect,
no wings to fly.
Take him as insane,
for this is a world of man!!!
Done.

In a Dark Cave

What a compulsion!
Time caresses my happiness in a dark cave,
precious stones decorate my dreams,
floating upon waves of pleasurable thoughts,
Ahh! Who allows light to enter?
Disintegrates the grand symphony of obsession,
I am the hearse of reality.

True Minds

A bare footed man walks along the pitch road,
at the height of Summer,
or the nude woman, my elderly sister,
running across the rooms of white palace,
feeding dolls like her lost children.

Heard the story from Grandma,
a man didn't speak for thirty years past,
defying death, yet lose in prayer,
morning and evening,
high fever couldn't stop daily visit to his factory,
located in an imaginary map,
in his semi-functional brain,
Oh sister, oh father!
What sadness leads you to such madness, or
as villages to bomber planes,
are we not victims of unknown enemies?
Or the defenceless towers of your true minds
are turned to dust by deep turmoil within?

Why not the dormant volcano in fragile human frames,
but fall if shaken to roots?
You see, an ill-clad, barefooted man,
in hottest month of Summer,
begs food in forced destitution
and carries the cross for our sins.

The Dance of Death.

Dashed against the wall,
my head is blown to smithereens,
when you said 'no' to me.
But I see,
in the fertile soil,
yes, I mean the organic matter,
brain dust watered by pituitary hormone,
there grows a small silvery plant.
On its each branches sit flowers
drooping their heads,
like the lonely child whose mom is away.
Silence reminds me of your kindness,
an authentic fragrance of separation
that brings to recollection
blessed moments spent together;
misery multiplied,
I grow into a large planet.
Here there is no air to breathe,
no sad music to blissfully wash you in tears,
that flow like rivers
but stagnant water smells of dead fish,
I am the cascade that is running dry,
lost in the dark galaxy, unknown,
I start my last stage show,
the dance of death.
You say 'no' to me!!!

Don't Dare to Dream

Eyes blinded by rays of powerful misunderstanding,
emotions vaporized miles away from ground,
heart burnt by terrible energy released from thy hatred,
soul declared dead in radiation poisoning,
trapped in the wreckage of broken relationships,
molten rock in guilt,
when I cry, “Don’t dare to dream again”,
I hear a forgiving voice…
“Blessed is he who remembers my name”,
Hari Om!

The Woman of the East

I

I am woman,
witness in the garb of a courtesan,
when our princely states, fell one after another.
Grand, generous, philanthropic *Vasantasena,*
but who was there to fathom?
Kings too busy in trade of inter-state jealousy,
or lost in the silken pages of
life's magnificence,
colourful fairy tales,
Pomp unimaginable, corrupting vision.

When the white came with the torch,
for upliftment of India
the nation, the mother of civilizations,
transfigured into the figure of *Rassundari Devi*,
disregarding social norms,
me the downtrodden,
fell in love with the *maya* of alphabets.

II

But why did I drill myself so painfully?
The tyranny of male folk?
No, it's a dream,
one day my sister would say it firmly,
if West is the brain,
East is the heart of mighty civilization.
Remember your quotable quote, Macaulay?
I am the East whom you strategically murdered!

But I *Preetilat*a couldn't endure.
Why should I? As you see,
the Phoenix in me
reflects the spirit of United Nations;
Your Black gods are tricksters
or deity of black magic,
Our Krishna or *Kali* stand for love and power.
I Madam Murmu, am the threat to the racist world,
I am woman, the woman of the East.

**Vasantasena - a prominent character in the ancient Sanskrit play Mrrchakatika*
**Rassundari Devi - a Bengali woman of 19th century who is identified as the author of first full-fledged autobiography in modern Bengali literature*
**maya-here used in sense of attachment or affection*
**Preetilata - a Bengali revolutionary lady in British India who dies for her country*
**Kali - Hindu goddess*

The Joystick

Out of the protection of dreams
when life attacks me smartly,
seven warriors around one,
Abhimanyu in the middle,
Preposterous,
I succumb to defeat,
Gliding from the higher zone of self-expectations
to the lower level of compromises,
What controls my movements,
sets my attitude and altitude,
offers me a controlled descent,
is your voice, my Lord, the joystick.
Hear the reverberations of thy song,
heard before or *deja vu*,
as love like light particles spreads out
like ripples in water.
Moving in dream!

Light and Shadow

When darkness works on me
like poison in entrails,
stabbed spine, broken bones,
raped genital left to perish,
I in half dead's agony
open my bruised eyes,
live long . . . live long . . .
remember the blessings of ripe hearts,
just then the serpentine cloud starts to breathe.

In the dusty storm,
desert mountains are blown off,
not the laboratories of lies,
the curtain of dusk descends fast
on my face, and I feel mom's tears,
"come back, come back".
What marvellous architecture is formed,
as light and shadow,
working in tandem, blood and tears,
as the baby sun
droops a little,
I lend him my colour.

Come on Mom, stand straight.

Tryst with Truth

I am a single, shimmering drop of tear,
sitting on your mind's first layer.
I have rolled down your cheeks
when you meet the girl,
a girl, eyes as beautiful as fairy's dream,
for long her parents have flown to God's abode! Woe;
a girl who floats like a bubble in the air,
with limited apprehension of the world,
lifting eyes from the story book,
whom you find going to the wardrobe.
Alas what you see!
Is she trying to recognize a particular odour
coming from olden clothes,
a folded shirt and a dated gown!! Woo.

Runs the mountain stream of wayward passion,
Alas! the tryst with Truth,
In wet eyes return wherefrom I came,
fountain of compassion.
True!!!

Friendship with Truth

We carry the symbol in our body,
thin shield of skin, defence against unsavoury,
as my friend is to me.
Yes, he protects me from the odds.
What is he to me?
Is he the spitting image of mine
or deconstruction of myself,
or the metaphor, Shiva's third eye,
representing higher consciousness?
If my friend is intuition and awakening,
let me wear him as my skin
for I have heard friendship
with truth means
becoming the best.

My Suffering

Happiness is shared
but who has ever come forward
to take a bite of that loaf called misery?
My suffering is my suffering,
my very own.
So, let me chew it,
enjoy every particle of it.
No mere unhappiness,
but deep sorrow,
yes, I can do it,
it's mine. Digest every bit of it.

And when happiness
searches for a drop of tear
in my room in vain,
I smile,
and you see
the smiling face of suffering!
Yes, that's happiness.
But if misery is mine,
happiness is certainly yours.

Winter

In a remote island,
far away from human warmth,
across the snow,
slide on their bellies
the upright Penguins,
endangered existence,
as reeling under betrayals,
our emotional selves.

Maybe that Bores is deeply dissatisfied,
paralysing our sensations,
therefore, this cold North Wind
has become strongest ever.
Alienation in the wind,
as if to bar the chill air of despair,
the casements of the white palace,
the dwelling of the couple,
masculine Sensibility and softest Mind,
are closed, eternally.

Here darker are the nights,
cruel passions thriving to throttle daylight.
From this white, dreary land,
how my penguin mind
wishes to fly away
to a green world
founts of love nurturing souls.
Alas! Me,
in this Iceland,
caught in the maze of spiteful indifference,
waits for the coldest death snare.
come back, my Love,
come back to me.

The Ultimate

Christ, my Lord,
selfless in heart as on the Cross?
A fleeting thought to perplex the woman
who believes none in the world is comparable
to the Supreme.
And here pride is punished
as with Medusa,
one should worship the ultimate,
neither the make-believe nor the mimicry,
is this why her admirers were turned to stones?

Standing all alone in the old church
where walls are wiser than priests,
she closes her eyes;
God,
thou have sacrificed thy only son.
Remember the selfless father Abraham…
But where is selfless love on Earth?
Yes, the moms.
The devout is about to move
with this pre-existent knowledge,
comforting to all.

But the walls have already started whispering,
the stone-headed fails to perceive
the difference between the husk and the grain!

Christ is Christ, the ultimate Teacher.

Flowers of Parijat Tree

For eon after eon the Queen has been waiting,
whenever the air caresses her tresses,
the floral odour balms her nerves,
agitated at the spectacle of human suffering;
fragrance of Leilani, in the air or
as suspended water vapours in the sky,
the poet in her, sees words,
tied to the legs of the white breasted swans
flying across the majestic sunset sky,
eyes refuse to rest!

Words are moving ceaselessly,
Heracles' task to join the opposites,
the dimensions of truth,
being shaped into an invisible garland,
decked with jewel-like stars.
The colloquial, the written or the literary form,
in the carnival of words, differences are dissolved.
Water vapours get condensed
and return to earth as shower,
poetry of the Master.
Here poet's passion is words,
condensed sensation, coloured
a perfect blending of thought and feeling.
Not like those who live in the ivory tower,
disseminating knowledge;
they are wise!

Some poets, like the aroma of *Parijat* flowers
mix in the hearts of humanity.
Blue carbon monoxide mixes with air
so does the sweet aroma of incense sticks,
let my mind burn the impurities of self,
and enter the souls of beggars
and the heads of the kings!
Janus faced sitting between work and devotion,
the Queen prays,
sublimate me into the aroma of true love
sans differences
only then will the fragrance of my poems
intoxicate you to say, Ah!
But I am proud philosopher and truth seeker,
the light of truth dazzles, you know.
Poet Angel, let my poetry be like you,
Soft, new light after rain,
neither heat nor hatred,
only surrender makes rainbow possible.
With what ease and lightness,
heavenly bodies create cosmological music!

Just like that,
let the reverberations emanate from my lips
as soft as rose petals,
lighten your mood,
like the last drops of rain
hang from the lowered eyelids of leaves.
For eon after eon the Queen has been waiting for,
for one true poem to make her immortal.

**Parijat - a flower of Heaven*

To a Blue Whale

A blue whale smilingly asks her,
"Are you ok? Are you happy?"
"Of course, am not a parasite to avoid
Predation",
replies the small, brown fish of tropical waters.

Frozen Memories

Depending on our disposition
we remember either the saddest or the happiest
memories of our past,
ruminate psychologists
but is there any rule?

The weird ways of memory are puzzling
for no one is a fool to look back,
as the weight of past slips
drowns one in the icy ocean of regrets.

Don't know why angels on a sunny day,
dip in the glassy waters of Manas Lake,
the mythic gateway to heaven,
when my mind piercing
the ancient blanket of drudgery,
enjoys the dream,
as life takes on beautiful forms,
but why then the lightning triggers
childhood pains, adolescent aberrations of broken
commands?

It's not as painful now as before.
Perhaps under pressure
they are converted into agate stones,
and see how it splits,
when the ray of conscious understanding
passes through them,
the seven colours of rainbow
bring into prominence
multiple subconscious recognitions
inviting change of perspectives!

So friends, in silence,
the sad memories may hide themselves fossil like
under the layers of alluvial soil,
your soft hearts or
the happier ones, unappreciated gems
within cavities in igneous rocks,
your tough minds.
No wonder that depending on our disposition,
we discover our
frozen memories.

Adieu!

Forced by inclinations,
Oof my naked pride!
I say adieu to my first love.
Alas! My poor soul, as free as a bubble,
thin walls of misconceptions evaporate soon,
released is my trapped ego, air of betrayal.

Under the Heel

Your lover for centuries,
over my chest, barefooted,
thou have danced to the music of creation,
and what a glory you earn!
Mother of civilization.

Yet, on the night of fun and frivolity,
changing your course,
you embrace a new path,
your new love.
The homeless mermaids cry aloud:
"come back, come back".

Ha! Though wish it strong,
or wait for another century,
can we return to our forsaken old selves?
No, I say to my dried tears,
believe it or not, the final journey is made,
here you see, dear lady, only acceptance.

Strange Bond

After decades I return to inhale your odour,
call you the schemer, a traitor,
for you,
the slave of Time,
the thrashing machine,
you disown past
like the seeds
from the stalk and husk.

Farewell, my dear city,
no longer mine.

Karna and Arjuna: A Dialogue

Karna: O son of Indra, my brother,
on the way of your "great journey" to the new world,
when the angel of death approaches thee as you fall,
the lamentations of your elder brother
have caused great commotion in the kingdom of Heaven,
a fact unknown to you till now.

Arjuna: But brother, think a little.
Aren't your sighs, the forebodings of the storm
that blows inside?
Weeps in desperation, your vengeful heart,
for your heavenly pleasure
should not be disturbed
by the possible advent
of your ever estranged brother,
the darer, the challenger.

Karna: Sadly even today
in your words I hear the sounds of discord.
Is broken into thousand pieces,
my heart,
for when you hate me, it's like
the razor-edged iron rods,
piercing the tongues and bodies of the holy monks
in the last month of spring.
No, no, I am wrong here.
The shafts, the stabbing swords
cannot touch
the bodies of renunciates.
But when dear ones hate me,
it's like the trenchant rod piercing open

a poisoned wound,
the pain is indescribable;
a deeper impact on my inconsolable psyche.

Arjuna: I am a noble warrior and
it's my eternal disbelief of my enemy.
Death has brought just an end to my body.
And the burden of memory,
seemingly, the greatest obstacle to the new beginning.
Come brother, let us drink together the water of Lethe.
Let us forget all the sorrows of the past existence.

Karna: Wait a moment.
When you call me 'brother',
it's like sprinkling holy water of love
on a consciousness shrivelled by lifelong offences,
an impious being destined to be sacrificed.
In highest moments of fulfilment, confusion prevails.
It's like oblation of water to my divine presence.
May the stone turn alive by your compassionate greeting!
All here have said to me:
"Karna, you are a tragic hero;
a draconian joke of fate, sardonic humour".
Yet as freedom eludes a wild boar,
hypnotized, he sits in the quiet of the cage,
peace, my restless soul;
rage in aching slumber.
wasn't it wise for me to wait for you then?
Only a conversation in private,
for only a hero can understand
and appraise another hero.

Arjuna: My analysis! Brother,
I am not 'Dharmaraj.'
Haven't you heard the causes of my fall
on the way of our "great journey",
logically interpreted, I hope, by
Yudhisthira, our brother?
Condemn me;
a profane mind torn by hesitations and doubts;
an incomplete journey
en route self-purification.

Karna: The way affection traps a mother's heart
in serpentine noose,
a man is equally caught in the net of doubts.
Still it is the norm that
goals should be set at the heightened plateau of highest ideals,
and if renunciation must be shunned as resignation in life,
is it disillusioned service,
the only way to salvation?
For other than this,
what else should bother me now?
Brother, perhaps your heart has been purer
than all and that is why
you were selected by His divine grace
to hear the 'slokas' of *Gita*.
How dare I, the fool,
to discuss in your presence,
life and salvation!
Oh gracious brother! Significant parts of your life
are spent in sacrifices and penitence –

once for breaking a pact with your kindred,
yet again to gain heavenly weapons.
And me,
driven by mother's neglect to the shoddy sheet of life.
As the hunt in the jungle,
Fate decides the course of my life.
The son of Radha,
blind devotion to friend brings me
kingship and its glory;
perhaps the negative attributes too,
acquired with time.
You brother, embody the blessings of a noble birth.
The best among the *Pandavas*,
thou outshine thy brothers,
Yudhisthira and Bhima.
Actions and reactions
reveal your character,
as to a blind, fragrance, the Champak flower,
a blossom on His feet, his *Sakha*,
you Arjuna not Yudhisthira, are
the recipient of his advices,
surmised in *Gita*;
When have you heard
Spring beautifies a dead tree?
My inquisitive self has already asked *Yamraj*,
"why?"
A rare combination of opposites,
he replies:
a hero and a renunciate,
on whom almost all depend for action;

a great warrior and a spiritual man,
a crusader for ethics and righteousness.
Then only I remember,
I must admit, your virtues.
Culmination of the lessons of the East,
you are *Syamantaka*, of Lord Krishna,
protecting the virtuous, terminating the evil.
Selflessness, your progeny, must learn from you.
No Achilles but only Arjuna could make it possible-
making the knowledge of warfare,
subservient to the prime interest,
wellbeing of all.
Grand warrior,
whose goal is perfection,
could never be proud.
Glory kisses his feet who subdues his pride.

Arjuna: You have surprised me brother.
You are the son of the Sun god.
Kunti, her majesty, is your mother.
Pandavas, the brothers.
Alas the History that punishes you,
forever pining for peace
that honour may bring.
Ha! the Sun that let you bear the burden
while in knowledge you grew, not all.
Oof! the humiliating call "Abhirath Nandan"!
You are eternally deprived.
Yet going beyond the cravings of life –
mother's love, brothers' affection, king’s glory,
you stick to your ideals, friend's duty to a friend,

sense of gratitude.
Sacrifice is the meaning of your life.
Let not appreciations embarrass you for
you have defeated all the provocations
unhesitantly, like a sage.
Tricked by gods,
donated even your life saving armature!
My brother, you are unparalleled.
Yes, Draupadi is my greatest sacrifice,
could never tell my brothers how I yearned for her
whole-hearted devotion.
Frustration, though boundless, doesn't eliminate desires,
rather it feeds the passionate hearts more,
as, never ending Sulphur and hell fire.
Rejection of Draupadi has certainly hurt your pride,
her grand presence among all, my expectations.
You see, during years of penitence,
breaking the vow,
I have married three princesses.
Fate has favoured me all along.
I am Arjuna, Krishna's favourite.
I am not Ekalavya, unlucky, hapless.
I have earned the favour of Guru Drona,
who refuses to teach you
without any fault of yours.
And the curses on you-
to lose your knowledge of weapons
when you need it most and that
your chariot would sink into the mud during battle and that
you would be killed when you would be most helpless –
perhaps have revealed to you much before your fall,

the machinations of Fate.
When was destiny in favour of you, brother?
That in her 'Swayamavar'
Draupadi declares you as undeserving candidate,
is also contrived by gods.
You are everybody's fool,
a cursed warrior,
descending from celestial heights
to the thorny planet
to court the mortal decree.
Relax.

Karna: No, you are mistaken as all.
Brother, you are *Kshatriya*, *Hastinapur's* pride,
not a commoner lamenting the enmity of Fate.
Is it wise to revolt against Fate?
Haven't I hated my destiny forever?
But what is Destiny other than,
the harvest of our action in previous births?
Piled up complaints gradually develop my pride.
I have seen Bhisma and
Gandhari Mata in Hastinapur palace,
inspiring examples,
see, how they do balance;
accept their Fate, yet conquering it by supreme values.
You get the rewards that humble nature brings forth.
It's not for nothing that to Draupadi,
you are the worthy disciple of Yudhisthira,
not the rest.
When have we heard that Wind disaffirms his strength,
Moon disavows her glory?
Nature revolts not

when in silence you accept the proposal,
your beloved, married to five husbands.
Silent were you
when lustful power disgracefully
stretches its hands to your wife's honour.
Shall I say you attained stoicism, dear?
A lover in heart,
yet a sage in control,
unlimited patience
fuels a hero's strength in the battlefield.
Though the heart weeps inward,
Gandiva waits for the opportune moment,
what distinguishes you
is your sense of balance.
You are the hero of *Mahabharata*,
one who is blessed by the Lord.

Arjuna: I Understand your indication brother,
yes, the Lord himself becomes my charioteer.
But it also, as I think now,
is a dictate of *Mahakaal*,
Eternal Time.
Fate is only one of his agencies,
No doubt.
Action, inaction,
unity, separation,
war, peace,
birth, death,
loss and gain –
aren't these all under his control?

Will you still value those
who attain things by virtue of character?

Karna: Brother you are on the wrong side.
Character is half your action,
half intention,
just like following the right ideals.
Ignoring this is ignoring *Gita*,
its thrust on action,
selfless action.

Arjuna: Yes, brother you have rightly reminded me.
Path of devotion and path of knowledge
are like just two sister rivers
to reach the ocean of light.
Salvation comes through either way,
followed selflessly.
The sailor remains unaware
how towards estuary
the waters of the three become one,
ultimate learning of mine.
Now I know, in His name
lies peace of mind.

Karna: Ha! Peace, the greatest illusion!

Arjuna: No brother,
Peace may come through meditation,
'Karmayoga' or as you said a while ago,
disillusioned service.
But see, with such knowledge

I fail to control my mind.
I have hurt you,
taking you for a perpetrator.

Karna: Brother, me too.
Even after death
propelled by my undying thirst for revenge,
I tried to make you understand in good words
who is better between us –
you or me.
Let me say why.
From the very beginning
deep hatred was nurtured in my mind
against the well-bred men of higher caste,
men of great descent.
The call "Charioteer's son"
was like pouring hot plasma into my ear.
Don't frown if I say,
Mata Kunti,
had associates in knowledge.
Bhisma and Lord Basudeva;
a shock indeed.
But before the great war came into certainty,
none came forward
to rescue the fallen star.
Bearing the cross all through,
Yes brother, you are right,
the only thing I desired
was honour.
Therefore, have fed the prince Duryodhana
with my boundless sense of gratitude,
but only to be left much lonelier inside.

To the epic poet, it's "heroic isolation",
but more painful to me
was my sense of alienation.
Never an exile could connect himself
with the earth he walks on,
such a rift is there between my physique,
my beautiful body with the gold shield,
the god gifted armour and earrings,
my birthmarks,
my Kashatriya spirit
and the harsh realities of servility.
Do you know Arjuna,
deep frustration and hatred of a crestfallen man
have marked you as my competitor
ever since the days of childhood?
Arjuna, you meant desperation,
more and more knowledge
only for the sake of learning, whereas
your brother had to lie,
move from Guru to Guru
to learn the arts of killing.
When you tried to develop yourself,
I degraded into false pride.
Mata Gandhari was right,
both Shakuni and I
instrumentalized the great Fall.
Brother, for you and Basudeva,
it was a war to dethrone *Adharma*,
my war began much before,
the caste ridden world must be perished,

the pride of Brahmins and *Khatriyas*.
No one notices the semi-clad young boy,
wandering aimlessly in the burning ghats.
In defiance, he spits repeatedly,
on the faces of the deceased,
the higher caste men and women.
Didn't I know which side was stronger or
who was going to win?
Yet went in vain the kind words of *Suryadeva*,
his repeated warnings and persuasions.
Imagine the helplessness of a father,
torn between his promise to the unmarried mother
and the son's resignation,
his resoluteness.
Can a father stop a son who is born
only to attain nobility in death?
Donated my armour and earrings to god Indra,
in disguise, your father;
No regrets,
though the wives' cries fill the air.
I signed the bond with death.
On her lap I receive what
I have aspired throughout my life,
Fame.
Brother, there's yet another reason.
Karna shouldn't seek mercy but
punish himself
for the wrong actions throughout,
otherwise he would have missed
the pride of death administered by you.
Brother, do your downcast eyes plead for forgiveness?

No brother, think a little.
How could I possibly take the sweet revenge
on my unrelenting mother?
Pooh! The knowledge of my imminent fall,
the greater truth
got stuck up
in the muddy soil of her mind in
such a way that
it slipped out of her mouth
only when someone poured cold water
on the pyre
after my mortal body was burnt.
But there's His justice,
Since then, every sensitive heart turns into
the urn where is preserved perpetually,
the ashes of my pain.
Yet, the pain is unbearable, brother.
Let us bathe together
in the river of forgetfulness,
to free ourselves
from the agonies of our past.
But please tell me brother
how will our souls be liberated,
free from the cycle of birth and death?

Arjuna: Brother, that we have come here
is also to return again,
in a new dress, to play a new role,
to fight a new war.
Salvation may
entail a whole life
or several lives, I believe.

Salvation is no mere 'enlightenment',
nor just awakening to the true nature of things.
Unlikely to come to you as abruptly,
as from the void emerges the deity to bless you,
as does Lord Shiva, after my prolonged *tapasya*.

Karna: Please brother,
help me to understand what you say.

Arjuna: Brother, I am not sure
but it may be so that
salvation comes with our attainment of true love.
Does wind or water say 'No' to impurities?
In sweeping romance they ignore variances.
In every birth,
we are to offer unconditional love to all,
love in which the differences are dissolved;
to realize His pure self
in 'Jivatmas'
at the end of the day, to be unified with Him thus.

Karna: But brother,
have you found anyone around us
offering such undifferentiating love to all?

Arjuna: Brother, think of Mata Gandhari.
Though plunged in grief
at the death of hundred sons,
she sees the righteousness of our actions,
the *Pandavas*'.
Her life is but selfless action.

Karna: But do you think
she was able to attain salvation?

Arjuna: Brother, only the Creator can affirm,
better we muse over her powers,
her power to curse the Lord.
Once Rishi Brighu cursed Lord Vishnu and then
Mata Gandhari, His 'avatar'.
Remember brother,
how she empowers Duryadhana,
before the war.
What is generally considered
as power of a bereaved mother
is originally the power of a saved soul
free from sin;
strong and resilient.

Karna: Brother, perhaps we are foolish
to logically understand
what must be perceived philosophically.
Truth eludes;
mysterious silhouette of thick mist
persists light of understanding.
Yes, Mata Gandhari seems to be
an enlightened being.
To her there was no difference
between one and the other
for all were loved in the same spirit.
But now when I think of Lord Krishna,
I further understand,
What is 'Mukti'.

Nothing is personal to him,
no loss, no gain.
Therefore, 'Moksha' is to be
in a perennially happy state,
in an ocean of misery.

Arjuna: But brother,
a question still haunts me.
Why Mata Gandhari receive
such a cruel death,
no favouritism from Fate?
Even Lord Basudeva is not spared.

Karna: Perhaps it is the rule of *Mahakaal*.
But, brother,
what I now think is
after a certain time
this realization,
like dew drop in heat
will definitely evaporate
and dream children,
playing on the shore of the ocean of melancholy,
again we are to start from zero.
In boundless yearning, man embodies the divine,
trees bear fruit,
buds bloom into lotuses with thousand petals.

Arjuna: Opinions vary dear brother.
Consciousness like ball may go on rolling,
carrying realizations of our previous lives

to our next births.
But to me,
starting from nothingness,
in each birth,
it is a fresh attempt to reach infinity,
this is what means it to be human,
till *Mahakaal* releases us
from the cycle of birth and rebirth.

Karna: Then brother,
on earth,
the only God to be worshipped
must be *Mahakaal*.
Brother, if not Fate,
Mahakaal is certainly God.

Arjuna: Brother,
I don't have knowledge of the supreme.
Perhaps Fate is God's controlling agency
and to me God
is also subservient to
the power of *Mahakaal*
as the created universe.
In different ages,
for different reasons
Lord himself
is to suffer the pains of mortal existence.
Who knows? Perhaps God suffers equally with us
and the answers of our unanswered questions
are lying in the depths of *Mahakaal*.

My brother, I understand.
Now, please come close to me.

Karna: What immense joy to hold you close!
It's like capturing the sky
in the confined space of my heart.
What completeness!
The fiery sun inside me,
seems to be extinguished in an instant;
a cosmic wonder.
Now it's time to pray in sleep while
deep darkness of tranquil nights prevail.
Like gods in meditation,
May my third eye awaken,
May peace descend on Earth.
Wondrous Peace!

Arjuna: Let us sit on our knees
and start praying to *Mahakaal*.
O *Mahakaal*,
May each of our human births be meaningful,
May we attain liberation
through knowledge, devotion, action and love,
love, that makes life truly beautiful.
Let us begin our new journey,
Amen.

As Soul to Heart

Are we here for a few days
only to cover and feed our poor little selves
then to stand one day in front of the mirror
for the anagnorisis, that
we are nothing more than degenerating bodies?
Lice sucking blood,
we move from continent to continent
Estragons and Vladimirs!
Here tramps are arrested and tortured
as rich burn money on lavish marriages!
My dear readers, don't you see
by default, life on Earth is unhinged?

Let us close our eyes,
and move to the compassionate blue star
as I have heard,
there human hands tinctured with sweat
create wonders,
a world where a little success is not ignoble,
rather you, the dwarf,
will be offered
a garland of nameless flowers of unsullied beauty
as the one formed by your firework,
may I say your fancy
on the flat breast of
irresponsible black nights,
breeding ground for lumpens and monstrous desires!

Let us go to the world
of innocent smiling children
bathed in pristine glories,
where truth to beauty is fragrant
like soul to heart
endowing earthly existence
with His magnanimity.
Brothers and sisters,
our sojourn ordains us not to despair
but hope for the best,
look at the mirror in sheer acceptance.

Hide My Shame

Hide me, hide me in your breast,
for absolute fear rules my eyes,
me, the Chandal woman
in love with the Brahmin priest.
May I ask, in which era is love free?
Cosmic irony.

Forced to choice, a girl is silenced
like the stale air of cemetery.
Glorious Sun! the warrior fights to possess me,
as my heart pines for the lover's soulful song.
Moon, the ethereal paramour yearns for me,
most unhappy a woman lies naked
to the piercing male gaze,
hide me, hide me, but who hears?

Ignorant was I,
your Dalit sister
when you assigned me the role of streetwalking
and didn't ask why.
I am the Nagar woman,
Every night I light the *diyas* for you,
O! arbiters of my destiny,
to camouflage- my moist eyes.
Hide me, hide me, hide my shame,
Do you dare to question my choice again?

**diyas - earthen lamps*

No Deliverance

Worst of my dreams
all the lies uttered to others
sit in a round
on the carpet of freshly mowed grass
and start introducing to one another.
That evening, all proud, think of itself the best,
innocent, fine, polished lies,
Kitty party of lies!
But why the two in in a corner
sitting in silence
stare at each other in dusky confusion.
When the moon waxes,
uncomfortable in silvery light,
all melt into air.
Yet the bulging eyes of the two
transfixed at each other,
trigger the blood in arteries
as I ask them, "who are you?"
A question is fired back,
"Who is heavier? Dead albatross or the lies we utter?"
Standing alone on the bleeding field of Karbala,
I hear thousand voices saying to me:
There's no deliverance,
No deliverance.
Sleep, man sleep.

25th December.

Sweet odour of essential lavender oil
didn't induce the labour pains
as the midwife spread a bedsheet
scented with the *itar* of misery for his mom.
Nothing unusual.

Deep grievances welcomed him,
a baby offshoot
of father's lust,
and malnutrition in the womb.
Look at him today,
how in tipsy sleep
he is lying on urban waste,
using Fevicol as adhesive
to fix his drunken dreams,
pockets of torn pantaloon
stuffed with expired lottery tickets.

Each evening his heart goes on fire
by the voluptuous billboards of semi-nude dancers.
Today on his chest hangs a cross
of God's son
who died for the sins of others!

A long queue on the lawns of the church
waits for free cakes
as someone shouts at the pickpocket,
"Son of a bitch!"
A sober one intones "forgive him today",
for the Lord
suffered for his ilk!

My Heart Bleeds

As I dive deep into myself
see only blood coursing through tubes,
fear that like a four footed,
all will get lost in the metallic smell of body fluid,
the vortex of thick, black coagulated blood.

Promises are not kept-
it's not like this unalloyed sorrow,
if nothing supersedes the pain of the mom,
the horror,
for the last time the darling babe
looks at her,
no sound,
indistinct, unclear, as of the deceased,
but silent tears ooze out of a dying heart,
sucking till its last,
with whom my
next door brother stops smiling;
infected prey of epidemic,
what about the unending wailing of unassured Hope,
sitting in the pensive heart,
in the disintegrating
light and shadow of burning *ghat*?

I wonder,
obscure in the abyssal darkness,
will I be able to meet that dot of light
shining like Moon on the face of the bereaved sky? –
unique is its lustre
lost at times under the veneer
of sentimental clouds
though the glow depresses even the king of misery.

Stopped his machinery of grief,
its intricate and baffling designs,
ruined is he, in his pride,
when true friendship kisses the smallest,
meanest honey-coloured mole,
the preserved beauty on the cleavage of the woman
waiting since Stone Age,
with her love intact.

Ha! Where are you?
Today my heart bleeds.

**ghat - in South Asia, a flight of steps leading down to a river*

Bouquet of Expectations

Sometimes I ask myself who am I?
Am I none other than my disoriented,
disorganised mind,
wherein flowers of expectations
do not wither away
though trampled a thousand times?

The nameless flowers, the shy beauties,
the lyricists, the singers!
with what passion they compose and sing,
their favourite song, the song of misery!

I ask myself:
"Am I just a bouquet of false hopes?"
Just now perhaps for the last time
the flowers tried to smile,
uninformed was my chaotic mind.

But I salute Musician of life
for regaling me with "Orchestra Pain".

Timid flowers subdued by one soft touch,
lie sprinkled on the dead bodies
of my false hopes.
What I am if not disordered, unsettled mind?

The Big Banyan

It's a story of ancient times.
In celebration mode,
entered into your parlour
a grey pigeon, faint-hearted,
that was just the beginning.

A prelude to the world of home,
a great flight to the world unknown.
Alas! The pigeon recalls with dismay
the salty freshness of sea bath
that became a relic of the past.

Like the blanket of a beggar woman,
or the morsel obtained in alms,
there was little that could calm
her ruffled nerves of recent past.
The forbidding shades of the big Banyan,
imperilled her haven of happiness,
from nowhere descended neglect,
as the grey pigeon was already forsaken.

Today in the comfort zone of your parlour
I see multihued feathers of some unknown beauties,
a call to you emanates from my weary lips,
rewinds the story of ancient times.
No way! what is lost,
is lost forever.

Smile on Lips

Only if the story were a little different!
spinning wind turbines,
restive men and women,
quiescent Job and Sarah,
you move on and on.

Yet persists the perpetual truth,
the unalterable reality,
long struggles, to perish miserably!
Oh Man! Won't you
cogitate what brings the smile of victory
to the lips of Destiny?

Ha, son of Eve!
Only if you don't fight and learn to seize!
Fire is eventually extinguished,
flowers shed their lives with smiles on lips,
as saints do in *samadhi.*

Modern men and women,
like the rivers forced underground,
attain glory in extinction,
go and hide silently inside buds,
to bloom or never unfold.

When Atropos comes to snap the thread of life,
just a contrariety, and
mounting on a smile,
defeat the biggest odd.
Only if the story were like this!

**samadhi - as per Hinduism and Buddhism, a state of intense concentration achieved through meditation*

Wish Fulfilment

My dear friend, just tell me,
is the hue of affection Blue,
as boast the heavenly sisters,
pure as they are, their blue bodies
worship the Sky in naked devotion.

But it's ok.
Life on Earth is garrotting.
Let us sail the boat of winged words,
let us quickly go to the world of blue fairies.

What do you say?
Is it the same in the world of stars,
the rules of the
Kings and the Ministers, and
worrying are the lots of the fallen and the enslaved?
Uh!

No, no. Act.
Those who have right to equality,
having eyes fixed on Earth,
please bring down the age-old stars,
when stars, over the hill, fall from the sky,
the dehumanizing structures collapse.

In the land of peace, peace is not a misnomer,
It's wish fulfilment, Aha!
Only then you say,
the colour of affection is blue,
not before that.

It is Fate

Only the star-crossed know,
There's something called fate,
that overpowers all.
When the suffocating smoke of confusion,
covers the face of Mother Earth with thermal clothing,
creation weeps asking,
"Father why have you put
all the irreconcilable strains worldwide,
in one gargantuan geometrical frame,
ocean of life?"
He says:
the children are sent to play a game of balance,
where the balancing mechanism is inactive by default,
And it is Fate, nothing else.
Now say,
are you ill-fated?

Pride of Modesty

Playing with the oyster
the girl suddenly finds a pearl,
white modesty quietly makes a home on her palm,
the girl wonders,
perhaps gentility is an ornament
of the best, or what?

Wide eyes ask the vast eternity
“who is the best?”
The waves, roaring like hundred lions, reply,
“Look at these oysters,
crushed by worldly forces,
yet uncompromising in virtues,
facing imminent fall,
quicksand under feet,
if in one such you see the pride of modesty,
take him for the best".

Now please tell me,
who has pleaded with the Moon ever?
Yet she tolerates the torturous Sun all day long,
but with downcast eyes in the semi-darkness of the
evening,
she comes to stand quietly on the eastern side of your
balcony.

Necklace made of oyster shells,
the girl looks upward.
The keen Sun doesn't notice the Moon
whose silent presence says to all,
being there is her only pride,
she says to herself.
Perhaps, just like these oysters,
the Best is
naturally humble.

It's Pure Joy

If my wish is like the white butterfly inside a prism,
standing outside, away from savage condemnation,
then I see the beautiful array of vivid hues
and say, fulfilment has its own colours.

It's joy for me,
when through the brown fog of metro-city,
I hear the music of eternity.

Joy comes raining down on my stale brain,
and the weary lips, innocently.

And it's pure as heart knows not
how to x-ray the dark interiors of dreary mind.

Ananda

Supplication of millions is often embarrassing.
My lovely friend, when you favour me not,
I become the reindeer,
running over icy terrains in dark.

More I pine for you,
thy delightful presence,
wearing an alluring smile,
moves farther and farther.

Hardly one hears a celestial voice through clouds,
swinging on the rainbow,
once in a blue moon, the divine beings
shower remedial petals over mortal discomfiture!

And when you bless me instantly
yes, when like the glow worm,
you come to me,
a mind, sinking in darkness.
Joy, my dear friend,
I hug you like a little one
Separated from estranged father.

But friend, amazing!
When I know you to be the offspring of
cosmological peace and harmony,
I become the supreme bliss myself,
and you call me then,
your *Ananda*!

**Ananda - extreme happiness, one of the highest states of being*

Joy and Sorrow

Whenever I try to square the accounts
I feel deranged.

The equation between
joy and sorrow,
weal and woe,
is puzzling.
Unhappiness is like sighs of a lover
on the terrace at twilight,
happiness is housewifery
in a modest one bed room flat,
like one rupee note slipped out of your hand.
Poetic sadness of the evening,
like warm clothes in Winter,
wraps you in compulsive endearment,
the heart camouflages a distressful ending.

Tell me please,
if misery is the only true friend of happiness,
or are these two marginalized prospects,
situated in polar distance,
with one last wish to meet in infinity?

Why then diamond mines are enveloped
in the colossal darkness of the dungeon?
Or will you say,
life on this globe is the biggest clock,
velocity makes its hands move enduringly
in the rooms of its two permanent tenants,
Joy and Sorrow?

My Bewailing Mind

Tansen, I have heard
that peacock doesn't strive to stand out,
it just unfolds slowly its magnificent wings.

Like that, bit by bit
the hues of your celestial raga,
the ecstasy of *Meghamallar,*
melt the hearts of craving gods.
To douse fire, they send lovely rain;
to quench the fire of doubts.

Tansen, it was your rebellion.
But don't dare to think that
Amritavarshini will soothe the flames
Raging in my howling mind.

Tansen, your raga *Deepak*
sets alight the *kundalini* of my existence,
reduces to ashes
the countenance of my private heart.
Be it absolute truth,
perfection or ultimate beauty,
miracle drugs are not always life-saving.

So, *Tansen,* please hold on.
Faiji, Vidyapati, Kalidas,
No, no, *Rahim Khan*,
I want to hear your *Dohe* couplets
to soothe the turbulence in mind,
just as the sweet sunshine of the next morn,
you may say, a well-wrought poem
by the Master poet,
relieves the bereaved minds,
after the night, death knocks the door.

**Meghamallar - Hindustani classical raga, a type of musical scale associated with the rainy season*
**Faiji, Vidyapati, Kalidas, Rahim Khan - eminent Indian poets*
**Dohe - Rahim Khan's famous couplets known as "dohe" offer insightful reflections on various aspects of life.*

Rarest Individual

Are you one of the rarest individuals
who keep promises,
I see your pen
unburdening your memory,
relieving the icy weight of grief
that blocks the gateways of mind
to fresh sensations;
one cleans walkways
after each snowstorm.

Are you the one who falls into fatal desolation,
yet not totally lost,
the one who sacrifices the comfort
to honour a pledge?

Mired in turmoil of unfathomable mess
yet engender rays of hopes
among the less fortunate souls
through selfless love,
but do tell who is true hearted
man or woman?

I know I am not.
My virgin mind is possessed
by cold North Wind,
croons my wounded ego.
My destiny is written in black,
A story of hidden desires, or ruptured trust!
Distance added to beauty that you admire.
Now, let me confess.
I am just the husk,
like snowflakes,
God's special disgust.
As meaningless
is the mimicry of glow-worms of stars,
so is my address,
lost, at my very birth.
I am Siberian blizzard.
apathetic to myself,
your distrust, your death.

Yet I ask you lofty mountains,
or you, the blue beauty, glacial meltwater,
heaven on earth,
are you dependable?

Then let it be so.
Not me but all the beauteous forms of Nature,
who abide by promises
in courage, forgiveness and selflessness,
be your love, but
only if you are the rarest individual.

www.ingramcontent.com/pod-product-compliance
Lightning Source LLC
LaVergne TN
LVHW010103110826
845155LV00028B/465

* 9 7 8 1 9 4 6 4 6 0 7 7 6 *